Contents

page

Say the sounds

ee igh oa oo ar
or ow ear er.

Fun at the market

It is fun to shop at a market!

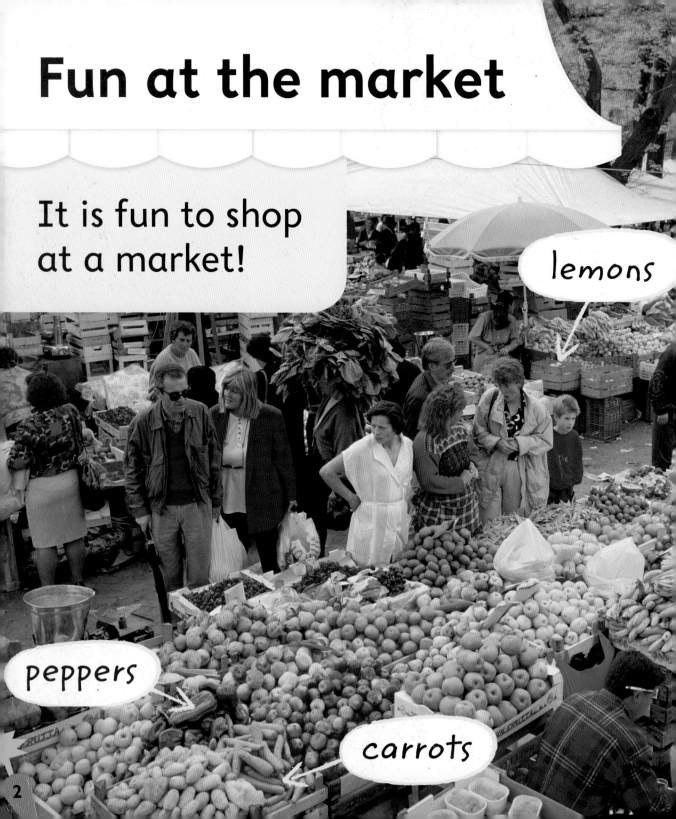

lemons

peppers

carrots

2

You can see lots of interesting things.

You can hear lots of things too!

apples

A farmers' market

At this market, all the sellers are farmers.

You can shop for carrots, beef, chicken, eggs or jam.

I might get this, it looks good!

A market on boats

This market sells food too.
All the sellers are in boats.

This market is in Bangkok.

The boats bob up and down a lot!

A fish market

This is a fish market.
Fishermen need to be quick
to get the fish to the market!

They need to sell the fish as soon as they can, or the fish will go bad.

Fishing boat

Art and books

Not all markets sell food.
This market sells art and books.

If you look hard, you might get a good book or a comic!

A sheep market

This is a sheep market.
All the animals are in pens.

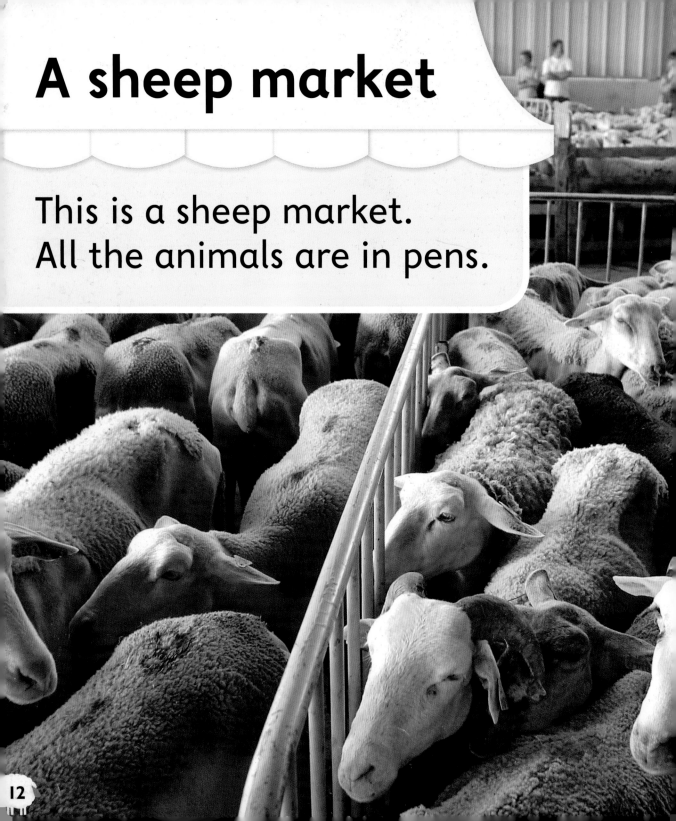

Farmers meet at the market and look at all the sheep.

This farmer needs sheep for his farm.

13

A camel market

This is a camel market.
The sun is up and the
camels are hot!

This man is checking a camel's teeth.

This market is too hot for me!

15

Index